The Olympics

Nick Hunter

WAYLAND

D0101909

First published in 2011 by Wayland

Copyright © Wayland 2011

This paperback edition published in 2012 by Wayland.

Wayland
338 Euston Road
London NW1 3BH

Wayland Australia
Level 17/207 Kent Street
Sydney, NSW 2000

Produced for Wayland by Calcium
Design: Simon Borrough and Paul Myerscough
Editor: Sarah Eason
Editor for Wayland: Katie Woolley
Picture researcher: Susannah Jayes

British Library Cataloguing in Publication Data

Hunter, Nick.
    Behind the scenes at the Olympic Games.—
    (The Olympics)
    1. Olympic Games (30th : 2012 : London, England)—
    Juvenile literature.
    I. Title II. Series
    796.4'8-dc22

ISBN: 978 0 7502 7065 6

Printed in China
Wayland is a division of Hachette Children's Books,
an Hachette UK company.
www.hachette.co.uk

The website addresses (URLs) included in this book were
valid at the time of going to press. However, because
of the nature of the internet, it is possible that some
addresses may have changed, or sites may have changed
or closed down since publication. While the author and
Publisher regret any inconvenience this may cause the
readers, no responsibility for any such changes can be
accepted by either the author or the Publisher.

Picture Acknowledgements:

Cover Main image: Shutterstock: Don Tran. Inset images:
Shutterstock: Eric Gevaert tl, Eastimages tr, Yan Ke bl,
Colman Lerner Gerardo br, Spine image: London 2012.
Back cover image: Dreamstime: Alexander Gordeyev.
Pages Corbis: Andy Star Mills/Ledger 4; Dreamstime:
Chungangus 15tr, Fstockfoto 18l, Guimahky 11, Kmiragaya
14bl, Mhryciw 5, Pniesen 26; Getty Images: 22, 27, AFP
8, 25, MCT 17, Sports Illustrated 19; Istockphoto: Maria
Toutoudaki 6l, VR Photos 7; London 2012: 1, 2, 10, 12tl,
12bl, 12–13, 13tr, 21tr, 28, 29; PA Photos: 20; Rex Features:
Sipa Press 9; Shutterstock: Geogious Alexandris 16,
Courtyardpix 24, Fstockfoto 18tr, Godrick 15br, Puwanal
6r, Chen Wei Seng 23, Sportgraphic 21l.

Contents

The world's greatest sporting event

On the evening of **27 July 2012**, the **Olympic flame** will be lit in the Olympic Stadium in east London, signalling the climax of the **opening ceremony**. Athletes from around the world will proudly parade through the Stadium in front of 80,000 cheering people. Each athlete will have trained for many years to be there at the world's greatest sporting event – the Olympic Games.

Olympic insights

At the Beijing Olympics the gold and silver medals were made out of silver, but the gold medal was covered with 6 grams of gold. 4,700 gold, silver and bronze medals will be made for the London Olympics.

Some of the US basketball team proudly show off their gold medals at the 2008 Games.

Hosting the Olympics

For the people behind the scenes, the opening ceremony marks a great achievement. **Hosting** the Olympic Games is a huge job and to get those athletes in the Stadium on that night in July 2012 takes thousands of people and years of work.

This book is the story of how the Olympic Games happen. Who decides when and where the Games will be staged? How are all the stadiums built? How do the countless tiny details fit in to the bigger picture?

Going for gold

The world's top athletes will hope to perform at their best to win those all-important medals. Some of them will be famous faces from recent Olympics, returning to the Games in the hope that they can shine again. Other athletes will come from nowhere to become stars overnight.

The lighting of the Olympic flame marks the start of more than two weeks of great sporting action.

Olympics by numbers

10,500 athletes will compete in London

20,000 journalists will cover the Games

One in three people worldwide will watch the Olympics on television

The Olympic Movement

The Olympic Games may have originated in ancient Greece about 3,000 years ago, but one man, Baron Pierre de Coubertin (1863–1937), is responsible for the way the 'modern' Olympics have developed. Coubertin was a French nobleman and historian who was passionate about sport.

Ancient Olympic Games

The ancient Olympic Games were first staged at Olympia in Greece in 776 BCE. These Games were held every four years and continued for about 1,000 years. The original site of the ancient Olympics was excavated in the late 1800s. In 1892, after reading about the excavation, Coubertin was inspired to revive the Olympic Games.

Sports of the ancient Olympics included short-, medium- and long-distance running races.

There were two javelin throwing events at the ancient Games: throwing the javelin for distance and throwing at a target.

Coubertin persuaded the Greeks to stage the first 'modern' Olympics in Athens in 1896. Only 245 male athletes from 14 countries took part but the event was successful enough to continue, and over time the Olympics grew to become the global event we know today.

The 'modern' Games

The 'modern' Olympic Games are held in a different city every four years and hosting the Games is a huge project in itself. The **Olympic Movement** is the name given to the group of organisations that ensure the Games are carried out according to the rules of the **International Olympic Committee** (see box below).

BMX racing was introduced as an Olympic sport in 2008 and is one of the newest sports to feature at the 'modern' Games.

Olympic insights

In 2012, London will become the only city to have held the Olympics three times. It held the Games in 1908, when it was the first host city to build a stadium specifically for the Olympics. Then, in 1948, while London was still recovering from the Second World War, it held the Games once more. Athletes had to stay in army camps and bring their own towels! In 2012, the **Olympic Village** where the athletes will stay will be just a short walk from the Olympic Stadium.

WORD FILE

International Olympic Committee (IOC): *runs the Olympics and decides where the Games will be held*

National Olympic Committees (NOCs): *represent each country within the Olympic Movement*

International Federations (IFs): *manage the Olympic sports, from archery to wrestling*

The winning bid

On 6 July 2005, **officials** from some of the world's biggest cities waited expectantly to find out if they would host the Olympic Games in 2012. Sporting legends, prime ministers and presidents had all tried desperately to convince more than 100 members of the IOC that their city and country was the best place to host the Games.

Olympic insights

London's aim in wanting to hold the Olympics in 2012 was to help young people to become involved in sport, just as British Olympic legend Lord Sebastian Coe had been inspired by the Olympics as a child. School children from east London were included in the bid presentation to make this point.

Huge crowds celebrated in Trafalgar Square at the announcement that London would host the 2012 Games.

The UK celebrates

The final vote had been between London and Paris. After the members had voted, Jacques Rogge, president of the IOC, announced the winner. The Games would be coming to London. The team behind London's bid celebrated, as did people all over the UK.

How did London win?

Winning the right to hold the Olympic Games is all about convincing the IOC members, who include Olympic athletes and officials, that your city will host the best Games. London's bid team put forward a proposal that included the regeneration of disused industrial land in order to create the Olympic Park, superb transport links to the site and excellent **venues** throughout the UK. The bid was championed by Lord Sebastian Coe.

Lord Coe (right) did not work alone in the Olympic bid — he was surrounded by a committed team of supporters including David Beckham and former British prime minister Tony Blair (left).

" London's vision is to reach young people all around the world. To connect them with the inspirational power of the Games, so they are inspired to choose sport. "
Lord Coe (Chair of the London Organising Committee of the Olympic Games and Paralympic Games), part of the winning presentation to the IOC.

Staging the Games

Once the Olympic Games has been awarded to the host city, the real work begins. The Olympic team has to plan everything for the Games, from building the venues to selling tickets to each event.

Delivering the Olympics

By the start of the Games, more than 100,000 people will be working to make sure the Games are successful, from government ministers to around 70,000 volunteers.

New sporting venues are built and old ones may be modified for the Games. Organisers must also think about what the venues will be used for after 2012.

Olympics by numbers

90,000 square-metres – the size of the Stadium field
860 metres – the length of the Stadium perimeter wall
532 Stadium floodlights

This is an artist's impression of the 2012 Olympic Stadium showing it lit up for evening events.

The opening ceremony of the Beijing 2008 Olympics was spectacular. London will have to come up with something equally amazing to impress its crowds!

A difficult job

There are other problems that have to be solved, apart from the issues of hosting so many sports and athletes. These include:

Cost: the Games are very expensive to host. The budget for the London Olympics is £9.3 billion, but this may rise to a much higher number by the start of the Games. The costs will be funded by a mix of businesses and government or 'public' money that comes from the taxes people pay.

Environment: venues and transport links have been planned to be environmentally-friendly, and existing venues and rail and underground networks will be used as much as possible to avoid new building work.

Security: organisers ensure the Games do not become a target for terrorists and other criminals by liaising closely with police throughout the event. Keeping people safe at the 2012 Games is estimated to cost as much as £1.5 billion.

Olympic insights

In 2000, the opening ceremony of the Sydney Games included a spectacular mix of fire breathers, jugglers and performers dressed as indigenous Australian plants and animals. Then, in 2008, television viewers watched in amazement as giant footprints outlined in fireworks appeared to walk across the Beijing sky at the opening ceremony of the 2008 Olympics.

Building the venues

When people think of the Olympics, they often think of the events held in the Olympic Stadium, such as the opening and closing ceremonies and the athletics. However, the Games are about much more than the Olympic Stadium. Many different venues will be used across London and in other parts of the UK.

Olympic Park

The centre of the London Olympics will be the Olympic Park, which is built on 2.5 square kilometres of disused industrial land in the Stratford district of London's east end. The Park will include the Olympic Stadium, which has been designed to hold up to 80,000 spectators at any one time.

The 2012 Olympic Stadium will be the biggest building in the Park.

The Olympic Park has also been designed to be a habitat for many different plants and animals. More than 4,000 trees and 300,000 wetland plants will be planted in the area.

The Park's eight other sporting venues are the Aquatics Centre, the Basketball Arena, the BMX Track, the Handball Arena, the Hockey Centre, the Velodrome, the Water Polo Arena and Eton Manor – a venue for wheelchair tennis.

Olympic Village

The Park will also contain the Olympic Village, where athletes will stay within easy reach of the main sporting venues. The Village apartments will provide accommodation for the 17,000 athletes and officials who will attend the Games.

Olympic cycling champion Sir Chris Hoy helped to design the Velodrome. It will house the Games track-racing events.

" The new Velodrome is going to be the best in the world. I can't wait until I can compete on it! " Sir Chris Hoy, three-times gold medallist at the Beijing Olympics.

Olympics by numbers

An Olympic-size swimming pool is **50** metres long and **25** metres wide. The Aquatics Centre for the London Olympics will have **two** 50-metre pools. The pools will hold more than **40** million litres of water and will be lined with **180,000** tiles. Water from the Olympic pools will be reused to flush the toilets.

Along with its two swimming pools, the Aquatics Centre will also have a diving pool.

Beyond the Olympic Park

The number of sports at the Olympics makes it impossible to stage everything in one Olympic Park, or even in one city. The 2012 Olympics will be using many venues outside the Olympic Park itself, and across the UK. Some will be built specially for the Games, while others that are already famous sporting venues, with a proud history, will be used for some Olympic events.

Olympic venues for 2012 will be located across the UK.

GLASGOW

NEWCASTLE

MANCHESTER

COVENTRY

CARDIFF

LONDON

WIMBLEDON

LEE VALLEY

WEYMOUTH

ETON DORNEY

HADLEIGH FARM

GREENWICH

Horse Guards Parade is normally used for the Queen's **Trooping the Colour** parade.

Olympic insights

Horse Guards Parade is usually home to the Household Cavalry, the soldiers who have protected the British monarch for hundreds of years. In 2012, it will be covered in 3,000 tonnes of sand to transform it into a sporting arena where 15,000 spectators will watch beach volleyball.

Famous venues

The All England Lawn Tennis and Croquet Club in Wimbledon, south west London, is the most famous tennis competition venue in the world and the perfect place to stage the Olympic tennis tournament. Although cricket is not an Olympic sport, the world-famous Lord's Cricket Ground in London will host the archery competition.

Many other parts of London will be transformed for the Games. Greenwich Park will become an arena for horses and riders in **equestrian** sports. Sports to be held outside London include the rowing events at Eton Dorney lake near Windsor and mountain biking at Hadleigh Farm in Essex.

A show jumping course with around 15 fences will be erected in Greenwich Park.

The enormous green space of Greenwich Park will provide an excellent venue for equestrian **dressage**, cross-country and jumping events.

Legacy

The Olympic Games are a great event, but each Games last for just 17 days. Organisers need to think about what will happen to the venues when the athletes and spectators are long gone. Venues such as the O2 (renamed the North Greenwich Arena for the 2012 Games), which will stage gymnastics, will return to their former uses. Venues that have been built specifically for the 2012 Games, such as the Velodrome and the Aquatics Centre, will be used by athletes and local people once the 2012 Games are over.

Symbols and ceremonies

The Olympics begin with the opening ceremony. This is a chance for the host country to impress the world with a spectacular display that showcases some of its culture. But the opening ceremony is also about much more than impressing the crowd. It includes many of the symbols that are an important part of the Olympic Movement.

Flag and flame

During the opening ceremony, the Olympic flag is raised. The rings on this flag represent the five continents of North America and South America, Africa, Asia, Europe and Australia, that are united in the Olympic Movement. The climax of the opening ceremony is the lighting of the Olympic flame, which represents peace. A **relay** of 8,000 runners will carry the flame around the UK, arriving in London for the opening ceremony. The last runner in the Olympic **torch** relay carries their torch into the Stadium and lights the Olympic flame in a special cauldron.

A torch bearer carries the Olympic torch to the opening ceremony to light the flame. The flame then continues to burn until the end of the Games.

The closing ceremony

After the final event of the Games, the closing ceremony takes place. The president of the IOC calls on the youth of the world to meet again in four years' time and the Olympic flame is extinguished. At the closing ceremony, the Olympic flag is passed on to the organisers of the 2016 Games which will take place in Rio de Janeiro, Brazil.

Olympic insights

At the opening ceremony, one athlete takes the Olympic **oath** on behalf of all the others. He or she promises to play fair and follow the rules of the Games.

A double-decker bus symbolising London's role as the 2012 host circled the Bird's Nest Stadium at the closing ceremony of the 2008 Games in Beijing, China.

London-Beijing-London

Olympic sports

Twenty six sports will feature at the 2012 Olympics. Being part of the Olympic Games can be very important, particularly for sports that rarely get the attention of mass media. Olympic sports can expect increased funding and **sponsorship**. So how does a sport become an Olympic event?

Athletes compete in a relay race at the 2004 Games in Athens. Athletic events have been regular features at the Games since the early Olympics in ancient Greece.

Changing sports

Some sports, such as athletics, fencing and swimming, have been part of the 'modern' Olympics since 1896. Boxing, wrestling and some athletic events were even part of the ancient Olympics. Many sports have been added since the first 'modern' Games. All sports featured at the 2008 Olympics will appear at the 2012 Games, but there will be women's boxing taking place for the first time.

Handball is one of the lesser-known sports to feature at the Games (see page 19). It became an Olympic sport in 1936.

The list of sports at the Games is decided by the IOC. Olympic sports have to be governed by an international federation and must be played widely around the world in order to qualify. Here are some of the lesser-known sports to feature at the Olympics:

BMX racing: riders need balance and skill to navigate the jumps, sharp turns and rough terrain of the course.

Handball: somewhere between football and basketball, this is the fastest of all Olympic team ball sports.

Rhythmic gymnastics: this is a form of gymnastics, in which equipment such as ribbons and balls are used in a floor gymnastics routine. It first appeared at the 1984 Olympics.

Olympic insights

The number of sports at the Olympics has increased steadily. The last Olympic Games in London in 1948 featured 19 sports – seven less than will be seen at the 2012 Games.

Olympics by numbers

2,000 athletes compete for just **47** gold medals in athletic events. **32** athletes compete for **two** gold medals in trampolining.

Water polo has been an Olympic sport since 1900.

The athletes

The 2012 Olympic Games will welcome athletes from almost every country in the world. Countries such as China and the USA will send hundreds of athletes. Other countries will send just a few. With just two athletes, the Caribbean island of Dominica was the smallest team at the Beijing Olympics in 2008.

Training for the top

Many Olympic athletes will be amateurs who have to work or study full-time as well as prepare for the Olympics. To stand a chance of winning gold, these athletes have to train for hours every day, often both early in the morning and late at night. Swimmers such as Michael Phelps and Caitlin McClatchey spend up to 25 hours a week training in the pool. Phelps eats more than 10,000 calories a day (almost three times more than the recommended daily intake for an adult male) to fuel his intensive training regime. Britain's teenage diving star Tom Daley has to study for his school exams while training for up to three hours every day.

Today, professional athletes can enter the Olympics, but before 1988 they were not allowed to compete.

> "It's every athlete's dream to compete at an Olympic Games but to have the chance to do it in your home country is just unbelievable." Olympic 4 x 100 metres medallist Mark Lewis-Francis' reaction to hearing that London will host the 2012 Games.

Mark Lewis-Francis fulfilled his dream of winning gold at the 2004 Olympics in Athens.

Village life

While competing at the Games, most athletes stay in the Olympic Village, which includes everything from shops and restaurants to medical facilities. The athletes' residential apartments will include kitchens, bathrooms and bedrooms. Regular, high-speed shuttle trains from the Olympic Village will provide easy access to central London in just seven minutes.

Athletes staying in the Olympic Village will be no more than 15 minutes away from the Park's sporting venues.

Olympic insights

Today, all sports include men's and women's events. This was not always the case. In 1928, some women athletes were so exhausted after the first Olympic 800-metre race, that no women's race longer than 200 metres was held again until 1960.

Elvan Abeylegesse is one of the greatest female long-distance runners of recent times. She won the silver medal in the 10,000-metre race at the 2008 Olympics, finishing the race in just 29 minutes and 56·34 seconds.

Paralympic dreams

On 29 August 2012, the Olympic Stadium will stage another opening ceremony. This time the crowd in the Stadium will welcome more than 4,000 athletes with disabilities to the Paralympic Games.

Paralympic history

In 1948, Dr Ludwig Guttmann held a competition for injured wheelchair bound servicemen from the Second World War (1939-1945) at Stoke Mandeville Hospital in England. The event was staged at the same time as the 1948 London Olympics. This event inspired the first full Paralympics in 1960. They were staged one week after the Olympics in Rome, Italy.

Paralympic athletes compete in 20 sports, including basketball. Events are managed to ensure athletes compete against others with similar disabilities.

Olympic insights

Wheelchair basketball players are incredibly fit and their specially-built wheelchairs use the latest technology and materials such as strong but light titanium. These wheelchairs cost thousands of pounds and they may only last for about six months. They are built for strength, speed and quick changes of direction.

Winter Games

The first Winter Paralympics were held in 1976 in Sweden with athletes from 16 countries competing. The Games took place in a different location from the Winter Olympics until 1992, when the IOC decided they would be held in the same place.

Paralympic athletes

Although the first Paralympians were athletes with spinal injuries who competed in wheelchairs, many other athletes with disabilities now compete at the Paralympics, including **visually-impaired** athletes and **amputees**. As such, Olympic organisers need to make sure that the Olympic Village and all venues are accessible to athletes with disabilities. All areas of the Village and the Park itself will have wheelchair access, and **Braille script** and speech recognition will be available on computers for those athletes who are visually- or **audibly-impaired**. With over 1,000 wheelchair spaces, the Park has also been designed for disabled spectators.

Olympics by numbers

Athletes attending the Paralympics:

1960 Rome, Italy
400 athletes from
23 countries

1980 Arnhem, Netherlands
1,973 athletes from
42 countries

2000 Sydney, Australia
3,881 athletes from
122 countries

2012 London, UK
4,200 athletes expected from **150** countries

The 2012 Paralympics will include athletic events such as long jump, triple jump and high jump (above).

Science at the Olympics

When winning margins can be decided by one hundredth of a second, athletes will use science and technology to gain any advantage that they can. The Olympic Movement must ensure that all athletes use equipment that has been approved by the IOC to ensure no athlete has an unfair advantage over another.

Starting blocks have sensors that tell officials if an athlete begins running less than 0.1 seconds after the start signal. This is then considered a 'false start' and the race is restarted.

Equipment and training

Sporting equipment is changing all the time. High-tech materials such as **carbon fibre**, which is light but strong, can help athletes such as cyclists to travel faster and therefore break records. The latest technology and materials have also made sports shoes and clothing more effective, which can help to improve an athlete's performance.

Drugs and sport

Use of illegal drugs is one way in which some athletes try to beat their opponents. Drugs such as **anabolic steroids** can help to build muscles. This is against the rules and most athletes are tested for illegal drugs.
As well as risking their health, drug cheats risk being banned from sport for life if caught.

Olympics by numbers

More athletes will be tested for drugs at the London Olympics than ever before. Urine samples from **5,000** athletes will be collected at the Olympic Games, and **1,000** samples will also be tested at the Paralympics.

US swimmer Dara Torres competed in the Beijing Olympics 50-metre **freestyle** swim wearing a high-tech bodysuit, and took the silver medal.

Split-second timing

Timing is one place where everyone benefits from technology. Electronic timing is used to find out who crossed the line first or touched the end of the pool first. This overcomes the human error problems of the past, when judges sometimes awarded first place to the wrong athlete. These days only the true winner takes the gold!

Olympic insights

Many swimming world records were broken at the 2008 Beijing Olympics where swimmers wore high-tech rubberised bodysuits called Fastskins. It is thought that the suits helped swimmers to move more smoothly through the water and to swim faster. In 2010, the governing body for world swimming, FINA, banned the suits because they could only be afforded by wealthy athletes, which gave them an unfair advantage over poorer competitors.

25

Media and merchandise

In 2012, millions of people from the UK and around the world will see the Olympics live in the Stadium and other Olympic venues, but most people will watch the Olympics only on television. It will almost certainly be the most-watched sporting event in 2012 around the world.

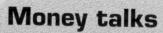
Popular events, such as track running, are closely followed by many reporters.

Olympics by numbers

4.7 billion people, or **70** per cent of the world's population, watched the 2008 Olympics.
94 per cent of China's **1.3** billion people saw the Games on television.

Money talks

Television companies pay millions to be able to show the Olympics. US broadcaster NBC has paid $2.2 billion (about £1.5 billion) for the rights to show the Winter Olympics in 2010 and the 2012 Summer Olympics to viewers across the USA.

The Olympics attract **advertisers**, too. At previous Olympics, some events have been timed to fit in with television companies' schedules, so that broadcasters in North America or Europe, for example, can get the biggest possible television audience. The Winter Olympics are now staged in a different year from the Summer Olympics. This is mainly because television companies found it difficult to persuade advertisers to pay for both events in the same year, but also to avoid the organisational strain of staging two Games in one year.

Raising money

Although media companies pay huge sums to cover the Games, this does not come close to covering the cost of hosting the event. Organisers hope to raise an estimated £2.5 billion by selling tickets and **merchandise** linked to the Games. They will also need sponsorship by large companies to help cover the costs of the Olympics.

Olympic insights

The London Olympic and Paralympic mascots are inspired by the UK's role in Olympic history. Wenlock's name comes from the town of Much Wenlock in Shropshire, where sporting games inspired by the ancient Olympics (see page 6) were held in the nineteenth century. Mandeville is named after Stoke Mandeville, the home of the forerunner to the Paralympics (see page 22).

Mascots Wenlock (left) and Mandeville (right) have their own blog, games and even a film on the official 2012 website!

After the Games

Every city that organises the Olympics hopes that the Games will have a lasting impact on their country. At the very least, the eyes of the world will be on them, and eight million people will travel to watch the Games from all around the world.

Inspiring future stars

London's bid to host the Olympics was built on the idea that the Games would inspire young people to take up sport. Many of today's champions can remember the day they were inspired to take up their chosen sport by watching a great Olympic performance. Dame Kelly Holmes was inspired to win a future gold medal after watching Lord Sebastian Coe win gold at the 1980 and 1984 Olympics.

After the 2012 Games, the Aquatics Centre will be equipped with a crêche, spectator galleries (below), family changing rooms and a café for the general public.

One of the 2012 Olympics' most important effects has been the improvement of a run-down London area. The Olympic Park will revive a wasteland area that was previously **polluted** and dangerous because of past industrial activity. The athlete's accommodation in the Olympic Village will be transformed into permanent and affordable homes for the public.

The Olympics will also leave the UK with some great sporting venues. The Olympic Stadium will be taken over by West Ham United football club. Track and field athletes will also be able to use the Stadium as a world-class venue. These sporting facilities will benefit local people and provide a base to train the Olympic stars of the future.

After 2012, ordinary people will be able to enjoy the open, green space of the Olympic Park within London's east end.

Olympic insights

The southern part of the Olympic Park will have riverside cafés, markets, bars and gardens. The northern area will provide a habitat for rare wildlife, including kingfishers and otters.

" This is going to do so much for our country, not just obviously the east end. David Beckham after hearing that London's 2012 bid to host the Games had been successful. "

Countdown to London

776 BCE the first recorded ancient Olympic Games are held at Olympia in ancient Greece

1896 Coubertin organises the first 'modern' Olympics held in Athens, Greece

1908 London hosts the Olympics for the first time. The Games take place in the first specially-built Olympic Stadium in White City, London

1924 the first Winter Olympics are held in Chamonix, France

1948 the second London Olympics take place. Europe is still recovering from the Second World War that finished three years earlier (1939–1945)

1948 the first Stoke Mandeville Games for injured servicemen and women take place at Stoke Mandeville Hospital, UK

1960 the first Paralympics are held in Rome, Italy

2003 the London bid team is formed to try to bring the Olympics to London in 2012

2005 **6 July** the IOC awards the 2012 Olympics to London

2008 construction begins on the 2012 Olympic Stadium and Olympic Park

24 August the closing ceremony of the Beijing Olympic Games. The Olympic flag is passed to London's Mayor as a symbol that his city will host the next Summer Olympics

2010 **9 December** Lee Valley White Water Centre is the first new Olympic venue to be completed. It will stage the white-water canoe slalom events

2011 Olympic venues including the Olympic Stadium, Velodrome and Aquatics Centre are completed

2012 **18 May** the Olympic torch arrives in the UK and begins a torch relay around the country

27 July the opening ceremony of the London Olympic Games

12 August the closing ceremony of the London Olympic Games

29 August the opening ceremony of the London Paralympic Games

9 September the closing ceremony of the London Paralympic Games

Glossary

advertisers people who draw attention to a product or service by paying the media, such as television and internet companies, to include positive information about the product

amputees people who have lost a limb

anabolic steroids drugs used to increase muscle size. Use of anabolic steroids is banned in all Olympic sports

audibly-impaired a disability affecting the ears and a person's ability to hear

Braille script letters that can be felt by visually-impaired readers so that they can read them

carbon fibre light, strong material

dressage an equestrian event (see below) in which horses perform movements such as trotting on the spot

equestrian relating to horses

freestyle discipline meaning that anything is allowed

hosting to stage or organise an event

International Olympic Committee the organisation that leads the Olympic Movement and oversees the organisation of the Olympic Games

merchandise goods, particularly clothing and other souvenirs that are branded or linked to a particular person or event, such as the Olympics

oath a promise

officials people who have a key role in the Olympic Games, such as coaches, managers and press-relation officers

Olympic flame a symbol of the Olympics that burns in the Stadium during the Games

Olympic Movement the name for all the groups involved in planning the Olympics

Olympic Village specially-built accommodation for athletes and officials during the Olympics

opening ceremony a ceremony that marks the start of the Olympic Games. Athletes parade around the Olympic Stadium in national teams

polluted made dirty or unclean. The environment can be polluted in many ways, such as by chemicals or litter

relay a race in which members of a team each cover part of the total distance

sponsorship to receive money from someone or an organisation in order to pursue a sport professionally. Companies may also sponsor events or people as a form of advertising

torch a hand-held object with a light or flame at one end. The Olympic flame is brought to the opening ceremony using a succession of burning torches carried by runners

Trooping the Colour a ceremonial parade of soldiers on horseback in front of the Queen

venues buildings or locations where something happens. Each Olympic sport takes place in a particular venue

visually-impaired a disability affecting the eyes and a person's ability to see

Further information

Books

Athletics (Inside Sports)
by Clive Gifford (Wayland, 2010)

British Olympians (21st Century Lives)
by Debbie Foy (Wayland, 2009)

Scandals (The Olympics) by Moira Butterfield
(Franklin Watts, 2011)

Sports Stadiums (Buildings at Work)
by Elizabeth Encarnacion (QED, 2007)

The 2012 London Olympics (Olympics)
by Nick Hunter (Raintree, 2011)

Websites

Visit the official London Olympics website to read the latest news about the Games:
www.london2012.com

The official Olympic website has lots of information about the Games' history:
www.olympic.org/ioc

Visit the BBC Sport website to find all the latest information and news about the 2012 Olympics:
http://news.bbc.co.uk/sport1/hi/olympic_games/default.stm

Index